Souvenirs and Homelands

Souvenirs and Homelands

Ken Cockburn

SCOTTISH CONTEMPORARY POETS SERIES

SCOTTISH CULTURAL PRESS

First published 1998
by Scottish Cultural Press
Unit 14, Leith Walk Business Centre
130 Leith Walk
Edinburgh EH6 5DT
Tel: 0131 555 5950 • Fax: 0131 555 5018
e-mail: scp@sol.co.uk

British Library Cataloguing in Publication Data
A catalogue for this book is available from the British Library

ISBN: 1 898218 93 5

The publisher acknowledges subsidy from the Scottish Arts Council
towards the publication of this book

Printed and bound by
Cromwell Press Ltd, Trowbridge, Wiltshire

Contents

III

Ken Cockburn was born in Kirkcaldy in 1960. He studied French and German at Aberdeen University and theatre studies at University College Cardiff. He has worked with various small-scale touring theatre companies in Wales; as a gallery administrator in Edinburgh (Graeme Murray Gallery, The Fruitmarket Gallery); and as Touring Officer with Readiscovery, Scotland's Book Campaign '95. He is currently Fieldworker with the Scottish Poetry Library, and lives in Edinburgh.

For Tamsin, Alice, Isobel

Acknowledgements

Thanks are due to the editors of the following publications, in which some of these poems first appeared: *Cabaret 246, Cencrastus, Gairfish, Lines Review, Markings, New Writing Scotland, Radical Wales, Spectrum, Squibs, Understanding, ZED²O,* and *The Ice Horses: The Second Shore Poets Anthology* (Scottish Cultural Press, 1996).

'Eurydice' was included in the pamphlet *Orpheus* (Red Sharks Press, 1988).

'Walking the Labyrinth' and 'The Necessity of Departure' were written for Paupers Carnival Theatre's *Desirable Residents,* 1990.

'Given: Seven Poems, Seven Days' was published as a pamphlet (Instant Republic, 1995).

Thanks also to the Scottish Arts Council for a Writer's Bursary, which enabled me to write some of these poems.

Eurydice

The sea's rhythms lull me awake.
Your breathing keeps time with the waves
which, imperceptibly, recede,
again to reveal hidden sands
as empty and fresh as my mind
from which yesterday has withdrawn.
I see the dawn on your hair
and on your sleeping face;
the slow transformations of your skin,
red diffusing to pink, pink
to the clear purity of day.
Endlessly the sun refines your features...
leaning over your mutable body
I kissed you, and you awoke.

I

Homelands

Abrasive, to imagine a poem
in praise of an abstract idea,
or an institution.

Cluttered Victorian monuments
(however nostalgia pleads)
these days are

plain unwieldy.
So please, no allegorical scene,
no mythic figure for a Continent.

Start instead with the specific –

A small city room, abroad perhaps,
a window away from the sea,
distant traffic, an old newspaper,

Riddle of dead fish in River Ely.
Shells in a glazed blue dish
on the windowsill –

These are fragments.
How are loyalties to be allocated?
Milton wrote, approximately anyway,

Truth came whole into the world
and has been scattered in a thousand pieces.
The Book of Genesis:

The whole earth was of one language...
let us build a city
and a tower, whose top may reach unto heaven.

Babel,
the atom
split by the LORD –

which fission liberated some
eccentric communions.
One story tells that James IV

had two children stranded on Inch Keith,
believing they might revert to Ancient Hebrew,
the language of Eden.

Eliseg's Pillar stands at Glyn-y-Croes
(or, as the monks would know it, Valle Crucis)
where Cyngen traced his lineage;

time has smoothed entirely his inscription,
are disappearing too the letters which
remember Lloyd, the pillar's

transcriber and its partial renovator
after Puritan demolishing.
The cross is gone, while the name lingers...

The unshaped Pictish stone at Abernethy,
one of many, whose apparent symbols
are now indecipherable –

With such forgetting, violent or peaceful,
such polluted connections, on what
is loyalty to be based?

Milosz – second hand again –
The impious man can walk for hundreds of miles
and not see anything which touches him.

Start instead with the specific –

Strange Hours

This room is a mess:
shoes, books, bottles, bags, letters, et cetera,
peering out uneasily
beneath last week's clothes
and somewhat longer's dust.

Hard to picture things when I arrived –
me, two suitcases by the door,
and aching shoulders unimpressed by
the morning rooftop panorama.
Bed, chair, table, lamp and wardrobe,
in a clean, functional, roofed space.
Then emptied, the suitcases – hup! –
(shoulders: that was stupid)
were stacked on top of the wardrobe;
whose well-designed shelves, racks and drawers,
little intricate compartments,
accommodate and classify
costume for varying climates,
seasons and social occasions...

These days,
the suitcases catch the sun
first thing.

Still dozing, I've lifted them in my dreams,
toward sometime uncluttered arrivals,
from almost unmanageable goodbyes,
in hot railway compartments after noon,
on cold railway platforms before sunrise –

when the alarm rings, as always,
the soothing pains in my shoulders
                    relax.

Self-Portrait AD *1500*

On a print of a self-portrait by Dürer

The room, the village, the summer,
were shared with that gaze, unnoticed;
but unobtrusively, gently,
and quite naturally
it slipped its way into my mind.
The latitude's remembered light;
a face upon the darkness,
every distraction lacking.

'Regard me as I regard you.
I'm not always this critical:
the eyes' clear gleam wasn't born of
anguished doubt, and I'd never have
worried these lips to such plumpness.'

Resilient, steadfast, self-contained,
I've read your pose is that of Christ,
with the hand held in a manner
specific (at the time) to Him.
For myself though, it seems to add
a sense of uneasiness
or vulnerability;
like a child clutching its blanket.
Skin touching fur, nail against hair,
the comfort of that which is now,
the firmness of the physical –
if the constant eyes bear witness
to succeeding generations,
such endurance is of this world...
'Regard me as I regard you.'
Serenity of his yearning,
an angel's sensibility –
quiet redeemer of the self.

Steam: in the showers
a fat man is whistling Bach,
lather in his hair.

An Old Poet Describes the New Poems

The new poems are everywhere.
They are memorable and subtle,
and often comic.
They complement an image,
as with Japanese prints,
and are concise as haiku.
Here is a new poem.
Imagine it overlaid
on blue sky and white clouds.

> It's not just a cloud. It's the start
> of a £3 billion production line.

This new poem troubles me,
for it describes
fixing the intangible,
valuing the elemental –
I dislike its propriety.
But, I am told,
such new poems are very popular
and more effective than the old ones.
They are read by everyone.
As a poet, I should be glad of this,
but the new poems trouble me.

Walking the Labyrinth

I know the way.
Up and down-stairs.
To the front garden, and the back.
I know where to go when it rains.

I know what's behind the wall, round the corner, over the road.
I know short-cuts and apple-trees.
I know necessary and unnecessary bus-stops.
I know which telephone boxes work,
     where to get a cup of tea,
     the shops selling Special Brew on Sundays.
I know zebra-crossings,
     where the subways go,
     which footbridges are advantageous;
I know where to go when it rains.

I can negotiate the one-way system.
I know the free parking spaces.
I can avoid a string of red lights,
I can get comfortable and not wake up the others.
I know where the buskers and the beggars go in winter,
     where to buy cheap socks,
     and where the unsold fruit is discarded.
I know the ledges where pigeons gather,
     and chimney-pots where seagulls screech at night.
I know of taxi-ranks and bramblebushes and shoeshops,
I know the dereliction of synagogues and Byzantium and
                 Father Jordan 'like the river',
I have deciphered carvings on tombstones and read the
                 plaques on park benches.
Once I gave nuts to a squirrel, and fell asleep in church.
I know where to go when it rains.

The Necessity of Departure

Here can no longer be home.
The Wall has been breached.
Within the Labyrinth, the Minotaur lies dying.
The situation has become untenable
and departure, a necessity.

Those to whom
our traces and our absence
pass, will they be haunted by us?

And how reliable is the map?
Don't expect me to
navigate by the stars.

On the Glasgow Bus

Early summer
commuting
two, three times a week
I'm struck out on the motorway by
how much I'm reading –
signs, numbers, slogans, names –
I copy them into a notebook
attempting a description 'in its own words'
of this place I'm passing
deliberately excluding myself:
with country this legible
so clearly defined and
(could one even stop)
closed to interventions
there seems little scope for a personal view,
access being restricted to emergency telephones
coloured orange
numbered 'SOS S1' to 'SOS S24'
sited at intervals between
'Clifton Hall School' and 'New Lanark'
although there must be gaps somewhere:
I've never counted more than twenty-one.

Garden Festival

Still fairly recently a place of trade
disposable, it closed and lay a while

unused, dilapidated, crumbling
an embarrassing eyesore, a hazard

finally requiring demolition
and ceding its space to a stop-gap car-park

as all around the city is remodelled
efficiently to exploit new business

by way of an encouragement to which
the thinking goes, this former place of trade

is made transitorily inviting
bread, flowers and circuses all summer

a riotous explosion of colour
transplanting memories of violence

and dangerous labour which also were
part of its heritage of industry

however the hatchets have been buried.

Radical Rap

War is the oppressor an aggressor no professor
war is the roar of the dinosaur
make you wet in a sweat when the bullet is a threat
make you forget the alphabet of that sweet jazz quartet

now all across Europe from Wales to Murmansk
you will ail you will fail unless people power prevail
from Reykjavik to Riga from Russia to Rosslare
dance to advance don't get entranced by high-finance

red wine white wine flowing like the river Rhine
I disincline to realign the force of nineteen eighty nine
no feudalism fatalism royalism racialism
rapping for community socialism!

1 958 Steine – Mahnmal gegen Rassismus

One thousand nine hundred
and fifty-eight Jewish
cemeteries, whose dead
absorbed in quieter
less hysterical times
lack descendants to be
recalled by, to walk with

Bordering on presence
the inscribed undersides
of cobblestones construct
this memorial to
invisibility

1 958 Stones – Monument against Racism – the title of a work made by the artist Jochen Gerz and his students at Saarbrücken Castle, Germany, in 1991.

A Flower for Hugh MacDiarmid

Taraxacum officinale

a composite plant with
jagged leaves and a large

bright-yellow flower on
a hollow stalk followed

by a globular head
of seeds with downy tufts

A Flower for Federico García Lorca

House-Museum Federico García Lorca, Fuentevaqueros, Granada

Visitors carrying suitcases, rucksacks,
and other objects of big size,
are not admitted.

Photographs may be taken in the patio,
but not inside the rooms.

Smoking is forbidden in the rooms of the house.
However they may do so in the patio provided they use
     ashtrays.

Food is not allowed inside the house,
though visitors may drink fresh water in the patio.

years of silence

a geranium flowerpot

remember his laughter

'In this town I had my first dream of remoteness.
In this town I will be earth and flowers.'

Souvenirs

A Selection of Street-Names
Adamsdown
Cardiff

Cone Incense
12 Kinds Assorted
Shoyeido & Co.
Kyoto

AGATE

COPPER

DIAMOND

EMERALD

GOLD

IRON

PEARL

PLATINUM

RUBY

SAPPHIRE

SILVER

TOPAZ

CHERRY

IRIS

JASMINE

JONQUIL

LILY

LOTUS

PINE

PLUM

ROSE

SANDALWOOD

VIOLET

WISTERIA

II

Flitting

Unknown
the questions such arrangements
answered

you shift things round so they suit

now the baby has the bedroom
we sleep in the ex-lounge and use
the old bathroom by the kitchen
– still with translucent windowpanes –
as study having already
stacked shelves with our own and others'
contemplations and histories

late sunlight illuminating
dust-jackets whose faded inks mark
similar afternoons elsewhere
this blurred outlook for want of form
reimagines and reinvents

snowdrop laburnum appletree
nesting martins migrating geese
the firth whenever the cloud lifts

Alice cries out in her sleep and
as if the sound of her own voice
consoles her immediately
dreams again rediscovering
moods and sensations which even
after only eight months afford
a vast complex panorama
her mind might relocate itself
within constantly anew
conjuring in its transgressions
alphabets and strategies for
unpredictable futures

now she sleeps silently on as
November darkness nudges me
away from the VDU's glow
towards my bed which has been made.

Reconciliations

The galleries are dark,
with renovation now imminent.
In the offices, themselves
about to be taken to bits,
archives are being boxed,
the morning's post is handed round,
the latest planning meeting's underway –
circumstance dictating rejigged schedules,
i.e. delay. The VDUs
blink beneath snow-dimmed skylights.

Come lunchtime, I emerge
into driving snow and keep my head down,
monitoring each footstep's progress.
There is no view of the city to be had,
a white-out. I stop off at the library
to drip-dry, return in unexpected sunshine,
arrive as massing snow-clouds, low, approach.

The VDUs blink,
the strip lights hum,
the fax emits irritating bleeps;
the latest draft accounts.
These I scan, obtusely, as daylight thins,
seeking, in their opaque assumptions, omens;
historical patterns,
current balances,
likely outcomes.
I feel a headache coming on.
I might be –
I open a borrowed book of poems,
the phone rings. Someone makes tea,
a warming distraction –

then early darkness, EXIT WINDOWS and
the monitors are switched off,
the strip lights finally.
The fax glows green and red. Outside
the wind has dropped, between clouds,
stars, all sounds
dampened by snow, the roads
are clear already, cycling
is feasible, I flick
the dynamo against
the wheel-rim to start
the journey, an inefficient system, yet
necessary, a distinguishable sign
of forward motion.

Redundance

The sun pours down on the overloaded hire-van.
These are the books wanted by no-one
being driven towards the dump.
I remember a teacher of mine suggesting
that excess information would in future
occasion greater problems than had, in the past,
a paucity of the same,
believing, I suppose,
in time's random selectivity.
Reversing towards the skip
I think also of book-burnings
but deliberate ignorance is not the same
as forgetfulness.
We establish a rhythm
launching unopened packages
into the space between
van-roof and skip-edge,
an action demanding
greater effort as
we move further and further
back inside the van
emptying it of
unprofitable knowledge.
Dust, sweat, hunger, tension
of muscles. We
target our throws away
from the centre, now
piled high
with burst packets.
Is this how Aristotle's works were lost?
One of the workers
directs me
round
the one-way system
towards
the exit.

Dolmen de Axeitos, Galicia

The roadsigns are uninformative. Instead of
the ancient monument our maps proposed
we are faced with sea. No calm lagoon or backwater:
the whole Atlantic's obscure enormous pulse,
colourless, white only on its broken surface,
pounding the rock of the peninsula,
its spray carried inland on the wind.

A paddle then being ruled out of the question
another holiday argument regarding
bearings, destination, whereabouts,
develops, though the baby's unconcerned,
happy in her here and now, until
possibly on a road connecting with
the main road or possibly elsewhere
a sudden arrow pointing into trees
informs us of the ancient monument.

Pebbles and evaporating puddles draw
the path on which Alice, learning walking,
totters, stumbles, stands and batters on,
mud staining the hem of her yellow dress,
deftly clutching a stone in either fist.
Around, pine-woods cede to oak, whose shadows
pattern dusty earth and half the dolmen.
The rest absorbs, like sponges water, sunshine.

A group of girls appears from I don't know where
of different ages, though none are older than
say fifteen, clamber onto the lintel-stone,
pushing, waving, giggling, calling for
la pequeñita in her yellow dress
who eyes them up. Lifts her arms, to say
she wants up too. The girls fuss over her
but she grips my finger tight and wants down,
moving to her mother who's peering underneath
into the stones' cavity, graffittied
like the roadsigns by language activists:
another wave of voices against the stone.

A path dithers through ferns towards foxgloves.
The shaded air fills quietly with rain.
The canopy of pine affords no shelter,
and, picking up the baby, we back-track,
running for the shelter of the dolmen.
The girls, already huddled, make room for us.
It's muddy underfoot, and I have to bend
to fit, but we're all out of the rain's reach.
Then someone notices the other kids,
the boys, who have taken refuge under ferns,
are soaked, and whose smiles express embarrassed bravado.
Another appears on a scooter, revs it up,
circles the stones and vanishes again.
As the downpour weakens to a drizzle, the kids,
both wet and dry, emerge to each other.
We follow them out. Translucent, a water-droplet,
leaf-suspended, one of millions, I touch
with a finger-tip. Released, a little stream
sets about exploring my skin's contours.
A second somehow finds a different route.

Alice in yellow squeals and does her dance.

After the Rain

Attempting to fine-tune the radio, here in the glade,
as sunlight flickers on sodden foliage,
is fiddly,
the station lacking a definite frequency –
but it's possible to establish that police
somewhere
have re-opened a 'missing-person' file,
on a disappearance 15 years ago.
No corpse materialised,
and the last known residence of the absentee
is rented these days by a man and his sister.
Recently
they bagged and dumped their old clothes and papers
determined, as they were, to forget the past,
move on.
Not a room in the house has curtains. After dark,
they stare at their reflections in the glass,
conscious
how visible they must be to those outside,
and wondering how to cope with another evening.
Eat?
One of their more ambitious compromises
requires from each, if food is being prepared,
no words.
Achieving thorough non-communication
is something they have dreamed about for years.
There is silence,
except for the nagging scrape of blade against whetstone
and the haphazard clatter of saucepan-lids and spoons.

If I had a hammer

A hot, dusty road leads uphill to a restaurant. The elder trees
have been brutally pruned, or simply broken. Little foliage
remains, and patches of squashed berries pattern the ground.

I share a table with John Smith, whose real name is Angus,
though goodness knows what his mother makes of the change.
We sit outdoors, taking our time over an extended meal.

Working with John on the hilltop, we perch on step-ladders by
a partly-constructed flyover, metal support rods jutting out from
concrete blocks. An unfinished spiral roadway ascends from
the town. John explains how most previous Labour leaders have
viewed the job as offering an expanded Foreign Affairs portfo-
lio, but he intends to expand the Prime Ministerial portfolio. He
demonstrates his ideas visually with two ring-binder folders,
the first full to bursting with documents, white originals and
pink copies, the second almost empty.

Below us stands Hugh MacDiarmid, who is wearing an old pair
of blue dungarees and odd shoes, one black and one white.
Thinking himself unobserved, he camps a little dance step,
lifting one foot and flicking it to the side. He then takes his
hammer and throws it with tremendous force down the spiral
road. The hammer bounces at regular intervals, each time
making a sharp *ping.* Following its progress, John and I turn
full circle on our ladders. The hammer bounces and sings, and
where the unfinished road meets a busy main street, it flies
through the pedestrians and the traffic into a residential side
street where its momentum fades and subsides in a wonderfully
resonant, harmonious, final sound. The crowds of spectators
who have gathered along its route break into spontaneous
applause. Hugh MacDiarmid is gratified and revels in the
appreciation though he recognises, it's exactly what he deserves.

Night Hymn (for Blinky Palermo)

Chimes spin through darkness   On their table
the catalogue is open at the essay
on Palermo's *undated scrap*
The sound of the child upstairs breathing
a steady rhythm on the intercom
cut by her cries until wound in sleep she settles
The writer quotes Novalis   *stories with no*
coherence and yet with associations, like dreams,
like so many fragments from the most disparate things
Her parents, out tonight, in the middle of
redecorating haven't yet hung blinds
Night, a dilated pupil, fills the window-
frame, gazing on bared plaster walls
that seem to be absorbing everything
A torn sheet of paper
watercolour silver bronze and pencil
slipped beneath a door in Copenhagen
twenty-odd summers ago to say simply
good night

Photographs

Sea-bathing at Bosa Marina
my eyes lifted from waves saw
                              fish
                    sprung on sea-pressure
                    arcing through air
                only to resubmerge
            as soon as
        seen, barely
afterimages
                              left.

Whim-picked snapshots fill three photo-albums.
Those discarded fill a cardboard box
ready for the rubbish. All are old
taken over ten years ago
when a student I had time to travel
like this one at Crantz near Hamburg, spring '81
an arch above a wooden gate, the text
inscribed on it restored as fresh as new
WIER HABEN HIER KEINE BLEIBENDE STADTE
SONDERN DIE ZUKUNFFTIGE SUCHEN WIR
The camera became unreliable
I travelled less and soon I found I'd stopped
fixing on light-sensitive paper those odd
afternoons, coming instead to favour
whichever scenes memory selected
to flicker on the eyelids' receptive screen
preferring such disconnected glimpses
tinted, faded and cropped by time as they were
to those isolated as they occurred
floating above the depths like dead fish
exact in each particular except
the sheen of the living thing lost.

'I'm afraid the time's getting on, Ken'
my wife calls from the next room, preparing
for work. I show Alice, two and a half
a picture in one of the albums of myself
taken around the time of the Crantz trip.
She asks me who the man in the photograph is.
CITIES WHICH ENDURE WE HERE HAVE NONE
INSTEAD WE SEEK THAT OF TIMES TO COME

Morgan

A ten-day haul through jungle
and Morgan's privateers
see Old Panama City.

Fled the rich, their riches, to
offshore havens
– nothing shipshape not
commandeered or spiked –

leaky fishing smacks bear
worked Potosi silver
to island shingle,
fringe of jungle

as smoke is creeping across the bay

but Morgan fixes it
for their return, only
in return unearths
every last stash

assuring his knighthood
and the Port-Royal governor's post.
To shore up law and order
he has stray pirates throttled.

Dead himself, storms
loosen his tomb and tumble it
into the scattering waves.
In Panama, six miles from the old,

a new city thrives.
Ruins
his only monument.

Reports from Haiti

1.

Once he had helped someone
someone with connections to
a literacy project.
When they called they said
we are cleaning the pot
and the little grains
that stick to the side
must also be washed off.
His wife recovered the body the next day.

2.

Processions crammed the streets, swaying, singing,
        whooping.
The crowds were playing crude but soulful instruments,
dancing and waving the leaves and branches of trees so thick
their parades looked like Birnam Wood advancing on
        Dunsinane.

3.

The ousted general flies into exile.
His forcibly abandoned properties
comprise a luxury suburban home,
a beachfront house about an hour's drive from
the capital, and his mother's home: each
is to be leased by U.S. personnel
and sublet to (unspecified) other tenants.
Market value rents are to be fixed
and paid to the general, who may
dispose of any assets as he will
from Contadora, a lush tourist island
lying off the coast of Panama
and selected as his place of residence.

4.

The mayor is on the bandstand, ready to address
a crowd of trade unionists armed only with brooms.
He cries, 'go and make our city ready!', and they
waving their brooms aloft disperse in teams
to shovel and sweep and bulldoze away the filth
that coats the sites of their suffering.
On each of the approach roads into town
platoons of men plant saplings in the dirt.

5.

It's uneasy, man, frightening.
We know the risks are always there
that they could hit us
any time.
I am still afraid of them
I still
sleep outside the area each night
because they know me.
I can't go home.

Flashback

Primed and released
        over Hitler's *Reichshauptstadt*

in turmoil and rubble
        the bomb was overlooked

as zero hour struck

as boundaries were redefined
        and millions moved to accommodate them

as the Wall was raised overnight
        and a generation of would-be migrants fell

as one night of joy led to
        slow years of disillusion

as streets began to be renamed
        buildings reconstructed

as navvies arrived one morning
        to excavate the foundations

        the bomb

primed and released
        over Hitler's *Reichshauptstadt*

suddenly remembered
        what it was capable of.

Reichshauptstadt: capital of the (German) empire

Higher

'Higher!' she shouts in the links
swing-park. I push into sound
erupting like a flood-tide
as trees explode crows and
arrowed from birches, a jet
repeats itself and repeats
itself and repeats itself
through clouds above the firth
and repeats itself again and
again until we distinguish
three circling warplanes
on some kind of training run.
Unbearable at first
it soon gets so you
stop even noticing the noise.
'Higher!' she shouts. I push.

Visiting

The birchwood's remnant edges
the new estate, home still
to rabbits who graze nightly
on whatever my father plants
till he fences off the beds.

Chrysanthemums grow now
and parsley, conifers
to screen the house from view –
in the six or seven years
they'll take to grow, you'd hope
he'll get on well enough
with neighbours not to mind –

Walking through the woods
Alice wants badgers, wolves,
elves at the very least.
She finds a dead sparrow,
talks about it for days.

Inside it's taking shape
their new home, with space
for us and anyone else
who cares to visit; yet
the presence granted me
is either formal, dressed
to graduate, be married,
or else displaced, old toys
kept for grandchildren's sakes.

Prior to the flit
I rummaged through the attic,
decided what I'd take
and what I'd no room for

but Alice clatters around
re-arranging dust-free
ornaments on the floor
with no sense of the past
and no sense of the future
making herself at home.

Keys

Departures entail the handing back of keys
you only ever borrowed, even if
the place was nominally yours. Return,
you'll have to buzz, announce yourself, convince
the keyholder you're not a threat, your voice,
flattened by the intercom's electrics,
belonging to another world, another stranger.

Oh, keys entail responsibilities.
At one time I had half a dozen bunches –
complications moving home and office –
they weighed me down, me worrying I'd left
the one I needed. No, better when, in transit,
I carried none at all, dependent on
acquaintances, on friends of friends, to open doors.

Spins and Turns

After the bells we'd had enough
of the country danceband's steady beat
and straightaway I found some jazz
that was nearer the mark: light, quick,
trying to catch itself out with spins and
turns dreamt up then and there.
I danced round the bed you lay on with
the end of the wine, that was nudging you
the other side of sleep
and you switched out the light, suggesting
I should switch off the radio too
but the music was suiting my mood, and besides,
then it stopped. The announcer announced
there was only time for one more number
and they'd do the *Doctor Kildare* theme.
I knew you wouldn't mind too much.
So I sat at the foot of the bed you were falling
asleep in, almost, but not, in darkness,
light from lampposts and maybe the moon
seeping in through the curtains, and I listened
as they revived *Doctor Kildare*
slowly becoming aware that
in front of me the lemon geranium
was oozing oxygen into
the atmosphere of the room, you know,
one of those meaningful insights that come
when you're half-asleep and half-pissed.
Applause. I switched the radio off
and joined you, gratefully, in bed.
Once I realised
I hadn't caught the band's name
I realised
I wasn't about to lose sleep over it.

Tuner

The broadcast voice   its lisping interference
wraps the room expansively as dusk
The window   now so little light's beyond
reflects the tuner's flickery display
the pauses and the emphases among
the closing roses   among the moths which contacts
imminent and current   will wipe to frenzy

Roundabout

On the roundabout, four flowering cherries.
At their centre a golden clock.
Blossom lavished like there's no tomorrow.

Then the roads were altered. Everything uprooted.
The clock returned, but not the trees, replaced
by shrubs, that don't stand out, that know their place
beneath straight-backed Time, a single point
of departure for countless drivers
anticipating mapped-out futures.

But trees recur. They bloom and leaf and fruit
and drop their leaves, their scented petals, on
whatever comes along.
It's too late, here, now. But if, elsewhere,
in motion, you reach a shaded intersection,
check your mirror, disengage the gears,
brake, halt the endless road a moment,
consider spring surrounding you
– its blossom, melled with crumpled wrappings,
lies strewn across the tarmacadamed grid
till, animated by a sudden, random gust
it rises up, a whispered revolution.

Clachtoll

What with the wind and the way the sand was sloping
the ball's soon rolling off towards the breakers
and I'm nearly off with the breeks and on in after the thing
but that makes it worse, the thought she might be stranded, so
it's back we turn and her still greeting, the fat pebbles
clattering under our boots, the ball away and
out of sight by now. She's happier
in with her gran. I'll away on my own.

At the far end of the bay I catch sight of the thing
wedged between rocks, a good few pools out from the beach,
then I'm slithering all over this bubbly seaweedy stuff
until I manage to reach, lay hands on, blooter the damn thing
                    shorewards
(so the arms can help with this not-falling-over slog)
but back on something the boots can grip there's no sign of it,
till along it bobbles on miniature waves in a wee pool,
all quiet and innocent-like, all 'what, me?', all wet.

Coat-flaps flying, she races out towards me
amazed and totally delighted something
so completely lost is (oh! and so soon!)
recovered –

Dun Canna

The winds are fiercer, once
the shelter of the hillside's
left behind; but the path
keeps going, right to the edge
where Dun Canna's tumbled stones
rattle underfoot,
a heap, their order all but
inconceivable.
The sunshine comes and goes,
seems more concerned with what's
beyond: the Summer Isles,
those hazy possibilities
out on the western sea.
A small boat's all you'd need
but here there's only ruins,
no means of setting sail,
of keeping yourself afloat,
the accumulated wisdom
as to undercurrents,
rocks and sandbanks, tides,
extant, no doubt, but not
accessible, these days,
now that the car's become
the obvious, the given
mode of transportation,
lines on road-maps forming
our labyrinths, the routes
that seem to lead to each
enchanted spot you'd ever
dream of reaching, till,
on leaning into the wind,
the stones, the sun, the isles
of summer whisper this
distinct possibility,
that magic's easily
ensnared by vanity –
Merlin, in the hawthorn-bush.

Patchwork Kingdom

Unseen my neighbours sleep.
Scissors and glue at hand
I rifle through piles of newsprint
for something or other I'd read
and thought maybe I'd keep
God knows where I saw it.
I'm struck instead by a headline
ship of dreams docks in Fife
Fife. Where I was a child
of gardens, playgrounds, beaches
and two bridges, one going north
the other south, that led
to all the places I reached
before here, a tenement block
on the other side of the firth
which my daughter knows as home.
On the other side of the window
moths, wisps of stuff
electrified by the light.
Hue of terracotta
a vase brims with buds
daylight will coax open.
A card leans against it
that my father sent my daughter
from Stornoway, on Lewis.
I'm working here this week
and I took a walk to the harbour
he writes, *and I saw fishermen*
mending their nets on the pier.
Poems, and dreams too, are stitched
on whatever thread's at hand
makeshift amalgams of
what's present, remembered, desired.

I'll hope to see you soon,
concludes my dad, concludes
the poem, ship of dreams
in whose churning wake, beyond
the sleeping tenement
beyond the one-way system
and the covered shopping centre
are gleaming, wave-reflected
like stars, the lights of Fife.

III

from

Given

For the Graingers

These poems were written at Downs Farm House, Yalding, Kent, between December 22 and 28, 1994. Each poem took as its starting point a word and a phrase chosen at random from a 'variable construction' by Gael Turnbull. These words and phrases are given in italics at the head of each poem.

With thanks to Gael Turnbull.

and there is no mistake (a look)

The year so far advanced
the train departs in darkness.
Beyond the station, moonshine
on one side of the sky,
sunrise on the other –
incongruous clarities
that fail to collide, as one train
flashes by another.
Dawn and the solstice, hinges
time and the mind hang on,
opening and closing in each
direction, unlockable, swinging
this way and that, in and
out, like the doors to the kitchen
of a busy restaurant,
made for mishap only
the waiters' poise averts,
a grace attained in motion,
stasis unable to reach
the like balance, stasis
a rabbit immobilised
by onrushing headlights. Startled. Stuck.
Can reflex move us in time?
Spinning away like moons,
like waiters, like small animals
gaining the darkened hillside.

December 22

for this day, and no more (a memory)

Darkness comes early, and frost with it.
Start afresh. Now. Leave
revising previous drafts. Let
tomorrow brace them. Here
stand something makeshift,
ephemeral, like, paper-lanterns, say,
mirrored in still water any
breeze, drizzle or ripple might
cause to vanish –
though here, illuminating
a single corner of the room,
light is electric (a desk-lamp
angled down), a pool
the tabletop, a notepad and
the lamp itself to some extent
float within. The floor
is porous to voices from below,
present and transmitted:
children, grandparents, animals.
I switch off the light and cross
the undulating floor, led
by what light pierces chinks
(effects of age or errors
of carpentry) in
the slatted wooden door.

December 24

compound of peacock dross (a moment)

Despite the mooted in-
corruptibility
of peacock flesh, its tail
stands as emblem of
the evil eye, or of
an ever-vigilant traitor.

The keep at Cardiff Castle
alone of many towers
played any military
role there, the rest
an 1860s folly
where sculpted creatures mount
redundant battlements
(although the strolling peacocks
were and still are real)
while inner rooms project
dynamic Victorian fancies,
Canterbury, Morocco,
Carcassone, fancies
a hereditary landowner
newly rich on coal
conceived and realised
in a florid imaginative
moment as ostentatious
as a peacock's fan,
perversely enduring as
the contradictions the bird's parts
occasion in phrase and fable.

December 25

that is and was not (a place)

The land was allocated
by certain documents
an owner, who wished to choose
for all those tenanted
upon that land, a priest.

Those whose families
had sown and reaped and sown
upon the land, themselves,
as other papers outlined,
wished to elect their preacher.

As a man of property
the landowner enclosed
his hand-picked priest within
the church, staunch and upright,
four stone walls and a roof

and those unpropertied
walked to worship beyond
the landlord's jurisdiction
on the windswept, wave-etched sands
between sea and the high-tide's limit

a place that is and was not
and was and is not a place

December 27